Introduction

CATS ARE A MYSTERY. That's true even after thousands of years shared with our kind and theirs. That's true even though we keep more cats as pets than dogs. And that's true even though we try our very best to understand what makes our cats tick.

Chances are, cats will always remain a mystery. And maybe that's the way we really like it. It's surely the way our cats prefer it.

And yet . . . knowing more about our cats helps us to bond with them better, care for them more appropriately, and love them even more.

Solving a few of those mysteries is what we set out to do in this book. We love cats—our own and all cats—and we want to help others to appreciate them more.

So enjoy finding out more about cats. We promise you'll be fascinated by the discoveries within these pages, and we promise something even more: no matter how much you learn about your cat, some things will always be a mystery.

And that, says the cat, is the way it should always be.

Dr. Marty Becker
Gina Spadafori

meow WOW

Curiously Compelling Facts, True Tales, & Trivia Even Your Cat Won't Know

Marty Becker, D.V.M., and Gina Spadafori
with Illustrations by Molly Pearce

Health Communications, Inc.
Deerfield Beach, Florida

www.hcibooks.com

Library of Congress Cataloging-in-Publication Data

Becker, Marty, 1954-

MeowWow : curiously compelling facts, true tales, & trivia even your cat won't know / Marty Becker and Gina Spadafori; with Illustrations by Molly Pearce.

p. cm.

ISBN-13: 978-0-7573-0622-8 (trade paper)

ISBN-10: 0-7573-0622-5 (trade paper)

1. Cats—Miscellanea. I. Spadafori, Gina. II. Title. III. Title: Meow wow.

SF445.5.B45 2007

636.8—dc22

2007032434

Publisher: Health Communications, Inc.
3201 S.W. 15th Street
Deerfield Beach, FL 33442-8190

Cover design by Larissa Hise Henoch
Interior design and formatting by Lawna Patterson Oldfield

There's nothing like a catnap

DOMESTIC CATS SPEND about 70 percent of their lives asleep. As you've probably guessed, most of those hours are spent in short snatches of sleep — catnaps, of course. That works out to be about sixteen to eighteen hours a day, or about the same as a newborn human baby.

Feline vitals

A CAT'S HEART NORMALLY beats between 140 and 220 times per minute, with a relaxed cat on the lower end of the scale. It's not unusual for the cat's heart rate to be high at the veterinarian's, because cats don't like being away from home, and they certainly don't like being poked and prodded by strangers.

You can take your cat's pulse at home, by the way. You need a watch that clicks the seconds off and . . . your cat! Put your hand over your cat's left side, behind the front leg. You'll feel the heart pulsing beneath your fingers. (If you can't, you might want to talk to your veterinarian about getting some of the fat off your cat!)

Count the beats while fifteen seconds click off your watch; multiply by four to get the BPM, or beats per minute.

While you're at it, you might as well check out your cat's respiration rate. Step back and watch your cat when he's relaxed and standing. Count the number of times the abdomen and chest wall move in sixty seconds. A normal cat takes fifteen to twenty-five breaths per minute.

Normal feline body temperature is between 100 and 102.5 degrees, read from a thermometer inserted where the sun doesn't shine.

The mystery of the purr

I T'S NOT A MYSTERY that caressing a purring cat is a pleasurable experience—it'll even lower your blood pressure. But what is a mystery, strangely enough, are the mechanics of purring itself.

In short, no one really, truly knows exactly how a cat purrs.

The most common explanation is that a purr originates in the voice box, with what are called the "vestibular folds," or false vocal cords. The passing of air across these structures is thought to get the engine running.

More interesting purr facts:

Purring is more than a sound of contentment. Cats also purr if they're injured, while giving birth—even when dying. British zoologist Desmond Morris has observed in his masterwork *Catworld: A Feline Encyclopedia* (Penguin USA) that purring is "a sign of friendship—either when [the cat] is contented with a friend or when it is in need of friendship—as with a cat in trouble."

Purring starts early. Kittens start purring even before they open their eyes, rumbling while nursing in what must be a reassuring sound to their mother—who's likely purring herself.

Little cats purr, but big cats can't. Your cat has one up on the lion: cats purr, but lions can't. (On the flip side, lions roar, but cats can't.) No big cat can get his motor running the way our household kitties can, purring constantly as effortlessly as breathing, both in and out. Tigers can rumble a tiger-sized purr-like sound, but on the exhale only.

Cats can't taste the sweet stuff

PEOPLE CRAVE SWEETS: cakes, candies, cookies, and sodas galore. But cats couldn't care less because the taste buds of a cat are incapable of detecting, appreciating, or triggering a craving for the foods we recognize as "sweet."

As "obligate carnivores"—meaning they need meat protein to survive—cats don't need to have much to do with sweets. It's unclear whether the ancestors of cats had the ability to detect sweetness and lost it, or whether cats never developed a "sweet tooth" because they didn't need it.

People eat a much more varied diet, and our

taste buds reflect that—we have nearly ten thousand taste buds on our tongues. No such variety for cats, who'd be happy to stick with small prey animals and need fewer than five hundred taste buds to figure what's good on the menu.

No doubt their limited abilities in this regard contribute to the well-known finicky nature of some cats.

Cats eat grass because . . . they like to

MOST PEOPLE BELIEVE THAT when a cat chews on grass it's because of an upset tummy. While that may factor into the urge to graze on some occasions, it's more likely cats eat grass simply because they like to. And the fiber probably helps with digestion.

It's not just grass, though. Plenty of other plants bring delight to cats. Many cats also appreciate alfalfa, rye, and wheat grass seedlings. You can keep your stem-chewing kitty happy by sowing seeds in a low, wide container and always having tender, young plants for nibbling on. Many cats also like parsley.

And don't forget catnip! Most people know about the amazing effect of catnip on many cats, but not many people know that valerian *(Valeriana officinalis)* also tickles a cat's fancy. Plant both of these in cat-proof areas or your pet may pull the seedlings out by the root! After the plant is large enough to withstand it, trim some of it and offer it to your pet.

Catnip makes some cats go crazy and mellows others out. But many cats aren't at all capable of enjoying the buzz—about half of all cats are genetically incapable of tapping into the joyful experience of meowie-wowie. And all kittens are immune to the "nip," with the ability to experience the catnip high showing up in susceptible cats around the age of four months.

Litter box problems often mean a sick cat, not a bad one

ASIDE FROM ROUTINE preventive care, the number-one reason cats are taken to a veterinarian is for what's called feline lower urinary tract disease (FLUTD).

Missing the box is a classic symptom of this serious illness, but many people don't recognize the fact that a cat is sick and sometimes resort to punishment (which not only doesn't work on a sick cat, but is also grossly unfair!). Cats with FLUTD can also be observed straining or crying in pain when they pee, and that pee can smell funny even to the educated human nose.

The disease can turn up in any cat, but tends to hit middle-aged, overweight pets most. Stress can also be a contributing factor, which is why the problem sometimes turns up when cats move, or new people or pets join the family. Keeping cats from becoming obese and encouraging them to drink more can help prevent problems, as can offering smaller meals and more play to relieve stress.

Cats with chronic urinary tract issues may benefit from a special diet. In any case, a veterinarian's advice can help keep a cat from contracting this top feline health problem or prevent it from coming back when it does.

Why cats get the zoomies

CATS WHO ZOOM AROUND the room for no apparent reason actually do have a reason after all: they're burning off excess energy. This is especially true for indoor cats who don't get enough exercise or stimulation by way of prey/pursuit play.

In the wild, cats sleep by day, storing up the energy for explosive chases when they're hunting their meals at night.

For house cats, though, hunting involves sauntering into the kitchen to kill a bowl of food—not much effort required. That excess energy still needs to be burned, usually somewhere around midnight when you're trying to sleep.

Tiger, tiger
burning bright

I F TOLD TO IMAGINE a "typical" cat, you're doing well if you think "tiger-striped." That's because the tabby stripe is the most common pattern in all of catdom. It's so dominant that even some apparently solid-colored cats can be discovered, on close inspection, to have faint stripes, especially on their heads, legs, and tails.

"Tabby" is a general term for striped cats, and in fact, tabbies come in many colors and patterns—more than forty varieties in all. Red tabbies seem to have a special following and mythology, perhaps because in male cats the red-orange gene is almost always connected with

tabby markings, while in females red-orange cats can be tabbies, tortoiseshells, or calicos. (About one calico in three thousand is male, but he's not your usual male in that he carries an extra X chromosome, an abnormality that not only makes him extremely rare, but likely sterile.)

Red tabby males are often called "ginger toms" with great affection.

Tabbies can be further distinguished by differences in the pattern of their stripes. For example, a spotted tabby has gaps in the striping pattern, making the dark color appear as spots. The most recognizable is probably the "mackerel" tabby, with parallel lines placed like the ribs of a fish—hence the name. All tabby cats carry a special mark in common—an M-shaped mark on the top of their heads.

The word "tabby," by the way, is thought to come from the word "atabi," the name of an ancient silk with a striped pattern.

Everything should smell like cat

WHEN A CAT RUBS against us, we accept it as a sign of friendliness and affection, which it is. But rubbing also performs a very important feline function: scent-marking.

Cats want everything in the world to smell like they do, and they spend their lives trying to accomplish that feat. When cats rub up against people or furniture, they're depositing sebum from glands on their heads to spread their own trademark scent on whatever they're bumping.

That's the most "people-approved" form of scent-marking in cats, but there are others. When cats claw, they're not only keeping the tips of their claws razor sharp; they're also depositing scent from glands in the feet. When they lick themselves (or you), they're putting scent-impregnated saliva all over. Smelling right to cats is so important that they'll even start grooming themselves after being petted, to cover your scent with their own.

The least popular—from a human point of view, anyway—form of scent-marking is urine-spraying. Although many cat lovers believe this to be a litter-box avoidance issue, in fact it's a completely separate behavior. A cat urinating in a box squats; a cat scent-marking with urine stands, backs up to the object he's intending to mark, twitches his raised tail, and lets it fly. Although urine-spraying is commonly a problem of unneutered males, cats of both genders, neutered or not, have been known to indulge in this messy, smelly habit.

Heads, you win

CATS' HEADS COME IN three basic shapes:

 Round heads, such as on the fluffy Persians;

 Triangular heads, such as on the sleek, show-bred Siamese and other so-called "Oriental" breeds; and

 Rectangular heads, such as on the burly Maine Coon Cat.

Most random-bred cats tend more toward the triangular head, albeit a less-extreme version than on show-quality Siamese.

Lionesses rule
and female cats do, too

I F YOU'VE EVER WATCHED a nature film featuring African lions—or even saw *The Lion King*—you know the lionesses are the pride's great hunters, but the males are first at the wildebeest.

That's generally true in cats, too. Female cats are better hunters—but male cats eat first and most.

Immigrants,
like most of us

CATS AREN'T NATIVE to the continental United States. Because cats have always been prized on ships for their hunting abilities, it's assumed cats came here about the same time all the other Europeans did, hopping off the boats and making themselves thoroughly and successfully at home.

Seek and hide,
kitty-style

CATS MAY BE TALENTED hunters, but for other animals—such as coyotes—cats can be attractive prey. The desire to watch the world safely is one of the reasons cats like small spaces. By curling up in a basket, box, or drawer, a cat can feel more secure.

Looking at it from the cat's point of view, the sides of a hiding space mean protection—a little cat-sized fortress—and a safe place to sleep.

Meowie-wowie

YOU WANT TO MAKE your cat happy, so you give him some catnip, right? Maybe, maybe not.

The ability to appreciate catnip is genetic, with cats about evenly divided in their appreciation of the herb. Maybe there are a few more in the "Catnip, good!" group than the "Catnip? What?" one.

For those cats that do appreciate catnip—*Nepeta cataria* if you want to be precise—the stuff produces different effects for different cats. But it's all good, at least for those cat who love catnip.

Nepetalactone is the substance that produces the mood-altering effect. Some cats get way mellow, while others get downright silly: rolling, rubbing, leaping, purring, and showing generally uninhibited happiness. The reaction is good for a few minutes.

Don't expect your kitten to get jazzed about catnip, though: the littlest ones (less than three months old) haven't the ability to get high, even if they're among the ones who'll do so later in life.

And don't worry that your cat will get addicted to catnip. It's considered safe, and it isn't thought to be addictive, so let your cat enjoy all he wants.

Want another plant that makes kitties go mmmm? Try valerian. Both catnip and valerian are easy to grow from seed, but the plants need to be protected while they're growing or your cat may rip them right out of the pots. Once the plants are established, cut fresh bits off and rub them on your cat's scratching post and stuff into toys. Bliss!

Feline-stein,
the college cat

STORIES ABOUT PETS THAT get come-ons from credit-card companies—or actual credit cards—are not that uncommon. But a cat with an advanced college degree? That has happened, too.

In 2005, a six-year-old black cat named Colby Nolan worked with a Pennsylvania prosecutor to catch two Internet scammers who were selling bogus college degrees.

Nolan ended up with a master's in business administration (MBA) from Trinity Southern University. Anyone who has ever gone through a real MBA program will envy the tuition—a mere $5,000. Despite not attending classes,

Nolan picked up a more-than-respectable grade-point average of 3.5.

Instead of heading into the job market, Nolan worked as "evidence" in the case against the company. It's said that when interviewed, Nolan remarked that the catnip on campus was plentiful. "I admit," he purred. "I inhaled."

Giving blood for a good cause

EVERY DAY, SICK OR injured cats require blood transfusions. That blood comes from feline blood donors.

The use of blood products for treating sick and injured pets has increased so dramatically that there is a growing shortage of canine and feline blood. Several commercial blood banks have opened in response to this need, and many veterinary practices have developed their own blood banks.

The donated blood is used in the same way that blood is used in human medical facilities: as whole blood, plasma, and packed red cells. The blood is collected in sterile plastic bags, and is handled and stored in the same way as human blood.

Cats don't get to volunteer for duty, but the ones who do give are generally pretty mellow about it. To be considered, they must be indoor cats between one and nine years of age, current

on vaccinations, with no health problems and not taking medications. There can be no kittens in their history (if they're female). They normally are given a mild sedative for the blood draw, and they can donate every three months.

Getting high

CATS LOVE HIGH PLACES for the same reason they like tight spaces—to give them vantage points that are both safe and allow them to watch the world. Their agility, balance, and strength allow them to get up into places we couldn't manage, but maybe it's their superior attitude that has them really appreciating that altitude.

If any animal thinks he's above it all, it's a cat!

If you're the kind of person who wants knick-knacks on every surface, it's not fair to resent your climbing cat for the occasional figurine hitting the ground and shattering into a million

unfixable pieces. Instead, compromise with
your cat: put your most delicate, fragile, and
valuable items behind glass in display cases,
and lock down everything else with putty
meant for that purpose. QuakeHold! or
Collectors Hold Museum Putty are two such
products.

Worship me,
I'm a cat!

MOST CAT LOVERS KNOW that cats were worshipped in ancient Egypt, where they were considered so important they were even given the mummy treatment and preserved for the afterlife. Thousands of cat mummies have been discovered in Egypt, and ancient Egyptians even shaved their eyebrows in mourning when the family cat died. But that's not the end of feline adulation:

- In Siam (today's Thailand), the cat was so revered that a cat always rode in a chariot at the head of a parade celebrating the new king.

In Norse mythology, Freya, the most renowned and desirable of the goddesses, traveled around in a chariot pulled by cats.

Of course, for every culture that appreciated the cat, there seems to be one that vilified the animal. Most notably, cats were thought to be linked to the devil during the Dark Ages, and many an innocent cat was killed, along with those people also thought to have connections to demons and witchcraft.

Deity or devil? In the end, it doesn't really matter. Through the ages, cats have proved their worth and then some, keeping critical human food supplies—grain storage and more—safe from marauding vermin. Maybe they don't deserve sainthood for their work, but they surely deserve respect and gratitude.

Friends for longer than we knew

UNTIL RECENTLY, THE CAT was commonly believed to have been first domesticated in ancient Egypt. But in 1994, archaeologists discovered the remains of a young cat buried with a person at a New Stone Age site (characterized by the development of agriculture and the making of polished stone implements) in Cyprus.

And now we're finding that cats have been around longer than we ever suspected. New findings show that curious wild cats first started snooping around grain storage in search of fat mice around 10,000 years ago, somewhere in what is now modern-day Iraq.

The animals were welcomed for their hunting abilities, and the Near Eastern wildcat *(Felis silvestris lybica)* is now known to be the ancestor of the world's 600 million domestic cats.

Up on your toes, pretty kitty

MOST CATS HAVE FIVE toes on their front paws, but only four of them hit the ground. The fifth toe is called a dewclaw; it is found on the inside of the front paw. The dewclaw is the feline equivalent of our thumb, and it's used for grasping prey and climbing trees. A normal feline back paw, by the way, has four toes that are all called into service when walking.

Any number of toes over the norm (usually an extra one or two, but occasionally as many as three or four) makes a cat polydactyl, which means "many fingers." Polydactylism is a dominant genetic trait, which means just one polydactyl parent is enough to make a litter of polydactyl kittens.

No matter how many toes a cat has, the arrangement of the paws is one reason cats have such an easy time going up a tree but such a difficult time going back down.

The feline climbing apparatus is designed for forward motion, which makes rapid ascent up a tree pretty darn easy for the average cat. Not so coming back down, which at best is an ungraceful maneuver of (hopefully) short falls, with a safe but embarrassed landing on terra firma at the end.

Frustrated?
Chatter, little kitty

CHATTERING IS AN INVOLUNTARY reaction of a cat who sees something she wants very badly—such as a fluttering bird or a feline enemy—but can't get to for some reason—such as being on one side of the window when the bird or other cat is visible.

If the keyed-up cat could pop her knuckles or chew gum to let out that extra energy, she would. By the way, a cat who's wound up is probably best left alone. A little redirected aggression could leave you with some nasty claw tracks on your arm! Sometimes when it comes to cats, it's best to keep your distance.

You say "hairball," we say . . . what?

TRICHOBEZOAR. That's the official term for a hairball, which really isn't ball-shaped at all but rather is more of an oblong mass of swallowed hair and gummy mucous. In all the world, there are few things more disgusting to step on in your bare feet at 2:00 AM, which is why your cat always puts them where you cannot miss the mess. (And who says cats don't have a sense of humor?)

The cat's barbed tongue is what makes hairballs pretty much inevitable. The tiny hooks pull out loose fur when a cat grooms, and the direction of the barbs means it's easier for the cat to swallow the hair rather than spit it out. Later, that hair comes back up in the familiar "ack, ack, blech" sound of a cat spitting up a hairball . . . er . . . trichobezoar, whatever.

Hacking up a hairball every now and then is normal. You can keep the number down by grooming your cat regularly to remove loose hair before it's swallowed, and by upping your cat's fiber intake by adding a little canned pumpkin or using a hairball formula food.

Counting the bones

WE CAN'T SAY FOR SURE exactly how many bones any particular cat has because a lot of cats have some anatomically unusual traits. A cat with a normal tail will have more vertebrae than a Manx with no tail, or a Japanese Bobtail with just part of a tail. No surprise that cats with extra toes sport a few extra bones, too.

The range for all cats runs between 230 and 250, with the average cat having 244 bones—about thirty more than humans do, by the way.

The skeletons of domestic cats are very similar

to those of tigers except that the chest is not as deep; there is a difference in structures at the base of the tongue, allowing the cat to purr; and the tail is more flexible.

The uncommon
calico male

ALMOST ALL CALICO (and tortoise-shell) cats are female, but not quite all. About one in every three thousand calico cats is a male . . . sort of.

Before we go any further, though, let's make sure we all agree on what we're talking about. A tortoiseshell cat has patches of orange or red and patches of black, chocolate, or cinnamon. Throw in a white background color—that is, a basically white cat with tortoiseshell patches—and you have a calico. Tortoiseshell and calico are not specific breeds of cat; they're color patterns.

Now that we're all clear, let's consider the genetics of cat coat color—a very complex subject indeed. The gene that governs how a cat's red/orange color is displayed is on the X chromosome. A female cat has two X chromosomes while a male cat has one X and one Y. Thus, any cat, male or female, can be orange.

In males, however, that color is usually expressed in one way: the tabby pattern, often called a ginger tom or marmalade tabby. It takes two X chromosomes to make a calico or a tortoiseshell, which is why the overwhelming majority of calico cats are female.

Every now and then, though, you get a male cat who has not only X and Y chromosomes like a normal guy, but also an extra X chromosome. This unusual genetic arrangement is called Klinefelter syndrome, and it happens in other species as well. If a Klinefelter male cat has orange/red coding on both his X chromosomes, he may be a calico or tortoiseshell cat.

In female cats, the red/orange color can be expressed in any of three ways: an orange tabby, a tortoiseshell, or a calico. People sometimes think that almost all orange tabbies are male, just as almost all calicos are female. Not true. For an orange tabby to be female is a lot more common than for a calico to be a male, and no special chromosomal arrangements are necessary.

Feline weight:
The big and the small

A N IDEAL WEIGHT FOR most cats is eight to twelve pounds. Even the larger breeds of cat rarely exceed fifteen pounds, with the exception of a few relatively rare breeds.

Some breeds of cat routinely weigh a few pounds more, without an ounce of fat on them. Among the heaviest breeds are Norwegian Forest Cats (who can weigh seven to twenty pounds), Maine Coon (seven to twenty-two pounds), Ragdolls (ten to twenty pounds), Siberians (ten to twenty pounds), and Turkish Vans (seven to nineteen pounds).

The Singapura is the smallest breed of cat, with females as tiny as four pounds (although they can get as big as five, and the boys can weigh up to seven pounds). The Cornish Rex, Devon Rex, and Japanese Bobtail are also feline featherweights, weighing in at about six to nine pounds.

The better to see you in the dark

A CAT CAN SEE in conditions that are more than five times dimmer than what we require, thanks to some fascinating evolutionary adaptations.

Long before a cat ever was caught in the headlights, the ancient Egyptians had another theory for why the cat's eyes glow at night: they believed the eyes of a cat reflected the sun, even at night when it was hidden from humans. We love that inspiring theory, but we have to admit modern science has given it a thumbs-down.

That flash of eyes in the night is actually light reflected back from a layer of special cells behind the retina, called the *tapetum lucidum*, which is

Latin for "luminescent tapestry." (We love showing off our Latin, even if we had to look it up first!) The retina is the light-sensitive tissue lining the back of the eye. Its job is to convert light into electrical impulses that are sent to the brain. The job of the *tapetum lucidum* is to catch all the light that doesn't enter the retina directly and reflect it back in, so every tiny bit of light can be processed.

Why? It gives this brilliant twilight hunter abilities that put night-vision goggles to shame. Add that reflective retina to the fact that a cat's pupils can dilate to three times the size of ours, and that they also have a larger cornea (the eye's outermost lens), and you can see why a mouse had better beware.

More about feline vision: All eyes have cells called rods and cones. Rods react to changing intensities of light, while cones react to color. A cat's eyes have more rods than we have, but fewer cones. This means that while we have better color vision, a cat can detect motion better. This, by the way, is typical of many predators.

Grooming,
by the numbers

THERE'S NO SUCH THING as random behavior when it comes to grooming. Cats have a pattern, and they follow it almost every time. Watch and you'll see it: Grooming starts when a cat licks her lips and then wets the side of her paw. She will then run the damp paw over the side of her face and behind her ear (like a washcloth), and then repeat the same sequence on the opposite side.

Next, she'll lick her front legs, shoulders, and flanks. Then it's one leg up, and then the other, to get to all those personal spots. The whole thing wraps up with a trip down to the end of the tail.

Grooming removes food odors from cats so

predators won't get a whiff of "What's for dinner?" Grooming also spreads the cat's own scent over her body, as if she has gone through a fragrant car, er, cat wash. Lastly, grooming, either her own body or others, acts to calm and relax the cat.

Tiger stripes are all the rage

THE MOST COMMON PATTERN in cats is the "tabby," a term that comes into the English language from the word "atabi," a silk imported to Britain long ago that had a striped pattern similar to that of the domestic cat.

Tabbies come in several distinct patterns and many colors, including red (more commonly called orange, ginger, or marmalade), cream, brown, and gray. The tabby pattern is so dominant that, even in solid-colored cats, if you squint a little you can often discern faint tabby markings, especially on the head, legs, and tail.

Tabby markings are a holdover from wild relatives. Striped fur provides members of the cat family with very effective camouflage in the great variety of habitats in which the cats live in, such as the jungle, grasslands, and plains.

There's no hiding from the veterinarian, though, even though the veterinary hospital is probably the one environment in which a cat would most like to disappear.

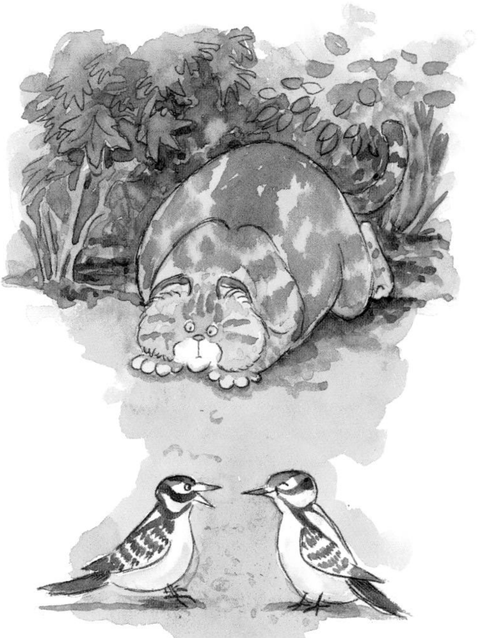

All-American cat:
it started in Maine

THE MAINE COON CAT is an American original. This hardy, longhaired breed developed as an all-purpose, all-weather New England farm cat and companion. The markings for which the breed is best known—a distinctively marked tabby—leaves the cat with a fluffy tail that somewhat resembles the tail of a raccoon.

Despite the persistent idea that the large cat came about because of mating with raccoons . . . well, hate to ruin a good story, but it's just not true. Nor is the idea that the cat developed from matings with North American bobcats. Maine Coon cats are all cat, and a lot of cat, for all that.

They also come in many different coat colors and patterns than the one they're best known for. This makes them share the same basic appearance with other large fluffy breeds, most notably the Norwegian Forest cat.

The All-American Maine Coon, however, holds the distinction of being the first breed to win the first major American cat show. That was in 1895, when a brown tabby female named Cosie won in Madison Square Garden, a place perhaps better known these days as the site of the Westminster Kennel Club dog show.

Perhaps that's fitting because Maine Coons are known to be easygoing and great with kids, among the more dog-like of cats. They're also the state cat of Maine, no big surprise, and originally earned much favor for their robust health and outstanding mousing abilities.

The better to ear you with

CATS CAN HEAR NEARLY three times more frequencies than humans can. For you technical types, a cat's hearing stops at 80 kilohertz, a dog's at 45 kHz, and a human's at a pathetic 20 kHz. Because cats can rotate their ears and focus each ear independently, they also can hear well from all directions. Kittens, however, are born blind and deaf. They don't begin hearing until about two weeks of age. Once a kitten can hear, though, she can hear things we can only imagine: bats in flight or a mouse in the brush up to thirty feet away.

A cat can rotate her outer ear to locate a sound—like the sound of a mouse's footsteps trying to sneak by—ten times faster than a dog. If that weren't enough bragging rights, a cat can hear nearly twice as many frequencies as a dog.

When white isn't right

NOT ALL WHITE CATS are deaf, but it's certainly not uncommon. White cats with blue eyes are more likely to be deaf than white cats with eyes of any other color. As protected indoor cats, however, a deaf cat can still be a wonderful pet.

Spraying: as normal as it is annoying

FIRST, LET'S DEFINE SPRAYING. When a cat squats to release urine, he's just eliminating waste. When he stands with tail aloft and vibrating, raising and lowering his back paws, and shoots a stream of urine straight back, he is spraying.

Spraying is not a litter box problem, although many people tend to lump it in with those behavior issues because urine is involved. But they're distinctly different behaviors. Spraying is all about marking territory.

Why do cats spray urine? While this behavior drives people crazy, for cats it's perfectly normal behavior. Spraying is the equiv-alent of posting a "no trespassing" sign, claiming territory from other cats, and mak-ing a place smell reassuringly like yourself (if you're a cat, that is).

Neutering before sexual maturity can help to prevent this problem, but not always. While tomcats (unneutered males) are the worst offenders, neutered males and even female cats will sometimes spray.

What about those baby blues?

CATS HAVE AS MANY DIFFERENT eye colors as adults—all beautiful, in our opinion—but at birth, all kittens have blue eyes. Kittens open their eyes at seven to ten days, but can't hear until they're about fourteen days old. If their eyes change colors, it generally occurs at four to five weeks of age. They'll start to darken as natural pigments are deposited in the iris.

Cats with points—light body color and dark markings on the ears, face mask, legs, and tail, like the Siamese—will keep those blue eyes.

White cats will have blue, green, gold, or copper eyes — or one of each. Other cats will have green, gold, or copper eyes, and those baby blues will change as they leave infancy behind.

A little Father's Day confusion

EVERY KITTEN HAS ONLY one mother and one father. But in every litter there may be kittens with different dads, because one female may mate with several males. And that's a good thing: any increase in genetic diversity and the potential for a successful pregnancy also increases the chances of survival of the species.

Forget the quick brown fox — cats can really zoom!

THE AVERAGE DOMESTIC CAT can run at a speed of around thirty miles per hour. Egyptian Maus are reportedly the fastest breed of domestic cat, capable of reaching thirty-six miles per hour. The American Shorthair is next, at thirty-one miles per hour.

To put things in perspective, the Thoroughbred is the fastest breed of horse, and can maintain a speed of forty-five miles per hour for over a mile. The fastest greyhounds run at speeds of just under forty-two miles per hour for about a third of a mile. But it's a cat that takes the land-speed record: the cheetah, which can hit seventy miles per hour for a couple hundred yards.

Like the cheetah—albeit not as fast—cats are built for quick bursts of speed. While you could never outrun a dog over distance, you could outrun a cat. They quickly overheat when running and have to stop after just thirty to sixty seconds to rest and cool down.

Before you outrun a cat, though, he'll probably be over the nearest fence. A cat can jump six
times his own length from a sitting position.
Their powerful thigh muscles coil and release
incredible energy, allowing them to escape grav-
ity and fly.

Did somebody say "diet"?

FATTEST CAT ON RECORD? Guinness World Records says it was Himmy the "Him-denburg blimp," a forty-six-pound male tabby from Australia.

With a circumference equal to an adult man's waist, Himmy's waistline, if he had one, would have measured thirty-three inches around. Now that's a fat cat.

Not a record to shoot for, either, because obesity, even of the Himmy record-setting variety, isn't any healthier for cats than it is for people.

By the way, if you have an overweight cat, you'll need your veterinarian's help on slimming down your feline fatty. That's because fat cats who go on crash diets can end up with a liver dis-ease that can be fatal. So proceed with caution on the slim-down plan.

You expect me
to eat that?

MOST HEALTHY DOGS WILL eat what you give them, but getting a cat to switch to a new food can be a challenge. But it's not really about being "finicky."

Cats are biologically programmed, learning as kittens to recognize certain textures, smells, and tastes as "food" and others as "not food."

That's why it's so difficult to get a cat to switch to a new product once you've found a brand and flavor he or she likes.

Here's another odd thing about feline

appetites: most cats are particular when it comes to crumbs—they won't touch them, unlike most dogs, who'll happily inhale everything put in front of them and then lick the bowl clean.

Mama cat, you are

CAT LOVERS ALL KNOW the special paw motions of a happy cat in the lap, although no one seems to agree on what to call this pleasurable bit of body language. Call it "making biscuits" or "kneading," the message is the same: affection and trust. Like a hug.

Making biscuits is a holdover from kittenhood. When cats are babies, they move their paws against their mother's side when nursing. When your cat does this to you, he's telling you he considers you to be just like his mother—purring and kneading in a demonstration of feline affection. It's a true compliment to the relationship you have with your cat.

Think they found homes for them all?

TEXAS TALL TALE or fantastic fact? The largest recorded number of kittens born to a single female: 420 (over the course of her lifetime). Dusty, a tabby cat born in 1935 in Bonham, Texas, holds this dubious and no doubt exhausting distinction. Nowadays, any good cat owner wouldn't be counting kittens but would spend his time counting the days until that spay appointment.

The mane event

THE MANE OF THE adult male lion is the only obvious sign of sexual difference in the whole cat family. Otherwise, male and female cats of all sizes look pretty much the same—at least from a distance.

Another difference between African lions and other cats: all other cats are solitary hunters. Alone among them, the lion takes a lot of pride in hunting in groups.

Make you a deal you can't refuse

WHY DO OLD TOMCATS look like the Godfather? With hormones percolating, one of the most visible characteristics is their puffy cheeks, which make them look like they have a wad of chew in each side. This is called "stud jowls."

Cats who are neutered before these develop never will get that "grizzled old tomcat" look.

Folding cat facts

CATS ARE ABLE TO squeeze through spaces that seem narrower than they are because they don't have a rigid collarbone to block their way through nooks and crannies. Once they can get their head and shoulders through, their sleek bodies present no further obstacle.

That's if those bodies are sleek, that is. The world is full of fat cats, after all, and for them, fitting through tiny holes is not a given. For one thing, they may think they're capable of fitting even if their paunch says otherwise. That's because a cat's whiskers—super-sensitive, specialized hairs—spread roughly as wide

as a cat does. But they don't grow longer as a
cat gets wider, which can lead some corpulent
cats into sticky situations.

Feline heat-seeking missiles

WANT TO KNOW WHY cats like to sleep next to humans in bed or drape their hairy heaps across our heads, legs, or torsos? Look no further than a clowder of cats (clowder is a fancy term for a group) and you'll often see them huddled, draped, or intertwined in a giant fur ball. Your cats just consider you a giant cat . . . or heating pad, if you prefer.

The desire of cats to seek heat can also get them into trouble. Cats have been injured or killed in clothes dryers after an unsuspecting human tosses a few clothes into a warm machine, slams the door shut, and hits the on switch.

Cats have also been caught in car engines after

crawling under the hood to snuggle against a warm engine.

During colder weather, you always need to keep an eye out for cats that are where they shouldn't be. Keep the dryer door closed and always scope out the interior, just in case. And for the cat snoozing in the engine compartment, a couple of hand-slaps on the hood will wake the sleeping beauty and send him on his way safely.

Feline fur facts

MOST CATS HAVE THREE kinds of hair in their coat: short, fluffy, insulating down; wiry, mid-length awn; and longer, straighter, protective guard. (The specialized hairs we call "whiskers" make up a special fourth category, the vibrissae.)

Not all cats have all three kinds of hair, and even those who do may have them in different proportions or lengths. The kinky-coated Cornish Rex, for example, has no guard hairs at all, and its down and awn hairs are crimped—as are the whiskers! The Persian, by contrast, has a straight coat in which even the down hairs are long by comparison to most cats, making the tendency to mat very pronounced.

A cat's hair is twice as thick on his stomach (120,000 hairs per square inch) as on his back (60,000 hairs per square inch). Sometimes it seems like we're wearing half of those hairs on our own clothes!

Meat is neat—
if you're a cat

THERE ARE QUITE A few people who for various reasons—health, religion, or an aversion to killing animals for food—won't eat meat. Some of those people, usually in the last group, believe it's possible for their pets to be vegetarians, too.

With some work, dogs can swing it, although it's certainly not recommended. Cats, though, need their meat.

Cats are what we call obligate carnivores, meaning they must have meat to survive and thrive. Among those substances found in meat that are essential to the health of cats is taurine, without which many cats would develop blindness and deadly heart disease.

No need to mess with perfection

DOGS HAVE BEEN CALLED the most plastic of species, ranging in size from Mastiffs that can top two hundred pounds to tiny Yorkshire Terriers and Chihuahuas, who don't even cause shoulder strain while being carried in a society dame's purse.

We've meddled plenty with dogs, but not much with cats. Among most recognized breeds, there's relatively little variation on the basic theme of feline.

Why the difference? Dog breeds have generally been developed with a job in mind, whether it's herding sheep, pulling sleds, or retrieving birds.

Cats, though, come well-equipped for the only task we've ever asked of them: keeping our homes and barns free of rodents.

Since they arrived pretty much perfect as they

are—just ask any cat!—we haven't meddled much. As such, cats don't vary all that much in weight or body shape. Variations on the feline theme typically show up in head shape, eye color, ear set, and coat pattern, length, and texture.

Belly up for protection

A CAT UNDER ATTACK who can't flee or bluff his way out of a battle with hissing and slashing may very well fall on his back to fight.

Why expose the belly to attack?

A cat in grave danger knows instinctively to engage his powerful rear legs and sharp claws in a raking action designed to tear into the vulnerable belly of an attacker. Think of it as inflicting eight knife wounds simultaneously and repeatedly.

Toss in those sharp fang teeth and the front claws working the opponent's face over, and, well, you've got yourself a warrior worthy of the ultimate fighting championship.

Whole foods are good foods

I F YOU'RE A MEDDLING momma cat, don't tell the kids to chew their food because cats aren't designed to chew. Rather, cats swallow their food and let their digestive juices process the meat, bones, and feathers. Whatever won't digest gets kicked out of the system undigested, either out the front end or the back.

The feline tongue is well-adapted to getting the most of anything that can't be swallowed: that sandpaper-like organ is perfect for scrubbing every bit of food off bones.

Meet the great hunter

CATS KILL THEIR PREY efficiently by biting their necks, spine or throat, or by crushing their heads with their very sharp canine teeth. (We bet cats hate the fact they have canine teeth!) Cats then tear off pieces of meat with their carnassial (tearing) teeth.

A cat named Towser eliminated a "cat's whisker" under 29,000 mice while being employed as the "Verminator Terminator" at a distillery in England. The pounce percentage for mousers: three pounces per ounce of mouse meat (assuming each mouse has about one ounce of meat), or one in three—not too bad of an average!

How many cats is that?

I F YOU DON'T SPAY your cat and let her breed as much as possible, how much are you contributing to the pet overpopulation problem? Humane societies, trying to promote spaying and neutering—a worthy cause, we agree!—have for years used the number 420,000. They say that's the number of cats who'll be around in seven years if one cat and all her kittens and all their kittens and all—well, you get the point—keep producing more and more kittens.

That number is on the websites, posters, flyers, and brochures of countless animal advocacy groups. And yet . . . it isn't really a valid number. We know because we asked Carl Bialik, who writes a column called "The Numbers Guy" for the *Wall Street Journal,* to take a look at the number and the assumptions behind it.

After talking to feline reproduction and population experts and then crunching the numbers, Bialik came up with a range of between one hundred at the low end and five thousand at the high end. Even the high end is a long, long way from 420,000. So where did the 420,000 come from? Nobody really knows. The best guess is that it represents someone's idea of what might happen if every female cat coming from that original hypothetical female cat had as many female kittens as possible as often as possible — and that they all survived and had as many female kittens as possible as often as possible. And so on and so on . . .

That doesn't mean you shouldn't spay and neuter your cats. It's good for their health, and it does help to combat the very real problem of homeless pets.

Even though one prominent animal advocacy organization told Bialik they'd take that 420,000 number off their educational materials, it still sticks around, rather like a homeless cat who has found a kind-hearted person who'll put out some food.

In the end, true or not, that figure is likely too imbedded in the public consciousness to ever really go away.

Fraidy cats?

A N "AILUROPHOBE" IS SOMEONE who is afraid of cats; it comes from the Greek word for cats. Ailurophobes become extremely stressed and anxious at the very thought of a cat, and can become near-hysterical in their presence.

Obviously, this is a mental-health condition that can be treated, like any other phobia. The word for people who just plain hate cats? We can think of a few suggestions, but one that doesn't apply is "friends of ours."

With more than 38.4 million U.S. households keeping some 88.3 million cats, we do believe we have those who dislike or fear cats on the run!

Oh, and someone who loves cats is an "ailurophile."

If you want fluffy, you'll pass on the Sphynx

OF ALL THE UNUSUAL varieties of cat breeds, perhaps none stands out more than the Sphynx, which is for the most part a furless cat.

Why do we say "for the most part"? These cats—who trace their origin to a cat born in Canada in the 1960s—do have some fur, although you might not recognize it as such. They have a sort of "peach fuzz" on their paws, tails, and toes. The rest of these cats feel like warm suede, and if you ever get a chance to pet one, you'll never forget the experience—your hand catches on the skin as you try to stroke them.

These rare cats are related to the Rex breeds—which have light coats of kinky fur—and come in all coat patterns. As you might imagine, the Sphynx cats do get cold, and need to be kept solely as indoor cats, with access to the warmer spots in the house.

Because skin, not fur, is the source of cat allergies, the Sphynx is not considered to be hypoallergenic. (No cat can be truly and absolutely so.) However, if you're allergic to the idea of picking cat hair off everything, this might be just the pet for you.

When in doubt, groom yourself

A CAT WILL START to groom himself at some pretty strange times. For example, a cat might start grooming when faced with an adversary who's itching to fight, or when getting into a tree after fleeing from a dog.

While these times may seem odd for pulling out a paw and starting to lick, they're a normal part of feline behavior. And no, it's not a cat's way of saying, "I'm so cool and you're such a fool that I'm going to groom myself right in front of you."

In fact, grooming in a high-stress situation is an automatic release of nervous energy, not a conscious act of in-your-face cattitude. Grooming is also relaxing and reassuring to a cat.

Think of it as the feline equivalent of a man straightening his tie before an important meeting.

We're ready for our close-up

PERHAPS BECAUSE THEY'RE NOT as easy to train—it's certainly not because of a lack of popularity—cats don't turn up in movies and TV shows as often as dogs do. Still, a few cats have done the star turn.

The first cat in the movies is said to have been a gray cat named Pepper, who appeared in a handful of silent movies. In the 1960s, Orangey, the marmalade tabby that appeared in *Breakfast at Tiffany's*, was celebrated for his supporting roles, which earned him two Patsy Awards, the animal equivalent of an Oscar or Emmy.

More recently, Himalayan cats have taken star turns: Sassy in the *Homeward Bound* movies and the cat that plays Jinx in *Meet the Parents*. The latter's work is a crucial plot element and a bravura performance from any actor, much less a cat!

Honor your mother cat

CATS ARE GENERALLY DEVOTED mothers. For proof you need look no farther than the story of Scarlett, the homeless stray who in 1996 saved her kittens from a burning building in Brooklyn, New York. Firefighters on the scene described to the media how the calico went back into the building time and again to save her kittens, even though she herself was seriously injured.

Firefighter David Giannelli scooped up the unconscious cat and her babies, and found help for them. He named the mother cat Scarlett, and despite burns severe enough that her ears were nearly gone and her paws badly damaged, she lived. She and her kittens were placed in loving homes.

Cats in the service of the country

THE BRITISH GOVERNMENT for many years kept cats "on the payroll" to help keep buildings free of rodents. The most famous of these cats have lived at 10 Downing Street, the traditional residence of the prime minister.

When the country's top mouser Humphrey retired in 1997 at the age of eleven, he'd been in residence through the terms of three prime ministers.

Speaking of British prime ministers, Winston Churchill was a legendary cat lover who doted on his marmalade tabbies.

Call me anything you want except late for dinner

CREATIVITY REIGNS WHEN naming cats, much more so than dogs. For one thing, the name you give a cat is pretty much between you and your cat. And because you're not really expecting your cat to come when called, the name can be as long and as fanciful as you wish. After all, as observed by T. S. Eliot in his *Old Possum's Book of Practical Cats* (which was the inspiration for the long-running musical *Cats!*) you can give a cat one name, but chances are your cat has a name he has given himself.

Lilian Jackson Braun, the bestselling author of *The Cat Who . . .* mysteries, made some observations about the naming of cats in *The Cat Who Tailed a Thief:*

" . . . [A] large percentage of cats are named after edibles: Pumpkin, Peaches, Sweet Potato, Butterscotch, Jelly Bean, Ginger, Huckleberry, Pepper, Marmalade, Licorice, Strudel, Popcorn, and so on.

"Names are not always complimentary: Tom Trouble, Stinky, Lazy Bum, Hairball.

"Cats named for famous personalities, real or fiction, are so named as a compliment to a namesake: Babe Ruth, Socrates, Walter Mitty, Queen Juliana, Maggie and Jiggs, Eleanor Roosevelt, George Washington.

"Cats in the same family often have names that rhyme: Mingo and Bingo, Cuddles and Puddles, Noodle and Yankee Doodle."

In our opinion, naming a cat is one of the most fun things about getting one!

Special veterinarians for special pets

D ID YOU KNOW THAT certain veterinarians receive certification as specialists in the care of cats? Like all specialists, those certified in feline care are called "boarded" because their over-and-above credentials are given by a governing board after the veterinarian passes additional requirements in study (passing a test), practice (serving a residency), or both.

Feline specialists are certified by the American Board of Veterinary Practitioners (ABVP). Those who pass the ABVP's certification will list extra credentials after their degree in veterinarian medicine. For example, after a "DVM" (doctor of veterinary medicine) you'll find "Diplomate (sometimes abbreviated as 'Dip' or just 'D') ABVP (Feline Practice)."

This extra effort to be so certified isn't the only sign that you have a great veterinarian for your cat, of course, but it usually does signify a professional who loves knowing the absolute best and most recent in medical thinking when it comes to feline patients.

Many veterinarians—both boarded and not—keep up on the latest in feline care by being members of the American Association of Feline Practitioners (AAFP). The AAFP also puts out materials that help cat lovers keep up with current veterinary thinking.

READER/CUSTOMER CARE SURVEY

HFMP

We care about your opinions! Please take a moment to fill out our online Reader Survey at **http://survey.hcibooks.com**. As a **"THANK YOU"** you will receive a **VALUABLE INSTANT COUPON** towards future book purchases as well as a **SPECIAL GIFT** available only online! Or, you may mail this card back to us and we will send you a copy of our exciting catalog with your valuable coupon inside.

First Name _____ MI. _____ Last Name _____

Address _____ City _____

State _____ Zip _____ Email _____ Comments _____

1. Gender
☐ Female   ☐ Male

2. Age
☐ 8 or younger   ☐ 13-16
☐ 9-12   ☐ 17-20   ☐ 21-30
☐ 31+

3. Did you receive this book as a gift?
☐ Yes   ☐ No

4. Annual Household Income
☐ under $25,000
☐ $25,000 - $34,999
☐ $35,000 - $49,999
☐ $50,000 - $74,999
☐ over $75,000

5. What are the ages of the children living in your house?
☐ 0 - 14   ☐ 15+

6. Marital Status
☐ Single
☐ Married
☐ Divorced
☐ Widowed

Hmmmm . . . did they forget something?

MAYBE IT'S BECAUSE CATS are so commonplace that it didn't seem necessary to mention them, but cats are the only domesticated animals not mentioned in the Bible. The Talmud has a lot to say about cats, though, all positive. In the Koran, cats are said to be the essence of purity. No surprise, we suppose, since Mohammed was a cat lover, as was Confucius.

In ancient times, cats were more than held up for praise—they were actually worshipped. As some have suggested, cats have never forgotten this and act accordingly to this day.

All cats are really the same — or are they?

WHILE ALL CATS SHARE many characteristics, in fact there are two distinct varieties of cats that come from different origins and do display some personality types unique to each group. (However, with so much accidental and on-purpose breeding over the years, the distinctions have been muddied a bit.)

The two types include: the lean, long, and agile cats of the so-called Oriental type, most commonly typified by the Siamese, and the heavier, less-active cats typified by the Persian.

Little ones learn lessons from Mom

FOR THE FIRST MONTH or so of life, kittens are helpless and vulnerable. Although their sense of smell works somewhat—they pick a favorite nipple on Mom early and stick with it—there's not much else they can manage. They seek out warmth instinctively at birth to help regulate their body temperature and stay close to the milk bar. Eyes begin to open at a couple of weeks, but don't work very well. Plastered to the head, their ears don't function very well. Tiny little legs don't help them to move, and if another den needs to be found for safety, Mom will do the moving.

And that's not all Mom will do for them. As disgusting as it seems to us, a mother cat will lick her kittens to trigger them to release droppings, which she eats to keep the nest clean. (People who bottle-raise orphan kittens stimulate and clean away messes with a warm, moistened cotton ball.)

As kittens grow, their mother starts to teach them what they need to know. If she's a good

hunter, she'll teach her skills to them, bringing in small prey animals for the kittens to chase. (Kittens' play behavior with humans is a form of this mock-hunting.) She'll also teach them a skill all cat owners appreciate: using a litter box.

We are Siamese
if you please

THE FIRST SIAMESE CAT in the United States is said to be a cat named Siam, given as a gift to Lucy Hayes, the first lady and wife of President Rutherford B. Hayes by the ambassador of Siam (the country now known as Thailand). Siam took up residency in the White House in the 1870s. These cats became highly sought-after in the United States and England, and they are now among the most recognizable of all cat breeds (even though other cat breeds now share the distinctive pointed markings, with darker fur on the head, legs, and tail).

Siamese cats became so well known that anyone over a certain age—think Baby Boomer—can probably offer up the lyrics to the Siamese cat song from the Disney classic *Lady and the Tramp*. (With DVD reissues, a lot of younger folks can do so as well, no doubt!)

Today, the appearance of the Siamese cat is controversial, with cat-show judges giving ribbons to exceptionally lean, long cats with triangular heads. Those who favor the traditional "apple-headed" Siamese—a heavier cat with a rounded head—have formed their own group to continue the look they love.

Egyptian adoration

IN ANCIENT EGYPT, anyone who killed a cat faced the death penalty. A little severe, no doubt, but considering a few of the animal-cruelty cases we've read about, maybe not all that crazy an idea.

The Egyptians idolized cats and even mummified them. One reason for the respect? The ancient Egyptians had a culture very much dependent on grain for food, and nothing can ruin grain storage more than an infestation of rodents. If you're hoping to protect your food supplies from vermin, a cat can be your best friend.

Territorial imperative, cat-style

L EFT TO THEIR OWN DEVICES, free-roaming cats in a neighborhood will delicately negotiate their own adjacent territories, or sovereign nations (feline-style), whose boundaries will generally be respected unless hunger or the urge to merge is present.

As anyone with cat-hating neighbors knows, a cat's idea of territory has absolutely nothing to do with such niceties as property lines drawn by humans. You can only make a cat respect human boundaries through the use of manmade barriers—such as keeping cats inside for safety and neighborliness, or erecting light mesh cat-fencing above the top of a standard fence. (If properly installed, cat-fencing will keep a pet feline in your yard, but it won't keep predators out, such as coyotes.)

The pioneering biologist Roger Tabor tracked the territory established by a neighborhood of cats in his book, *Cat Behavior*. He found that, left to their own devices, cats in urban areas will tolerate densities of up to fifty cats per acre. Within that zone, unneutered male cats will claim the largest territory for their own—about half an acre—while spayed females need almost no territory at all, being mostly content to stay very near their owner's home.

Country cats, he found, preferred to spread themselves far and wide—a density of about one hundred times lower than city cats.

Buy this . . .
or I'll snub you!

CATS MAY NOT BE as common in movies or TV shows as dogs are — or even horses, for that matter — but they're very popular when it comes to advertising.

Cats — and especially kittens — have been used since the earliest days of modern advertising to promote sales of everything from soda to lingerie — and cat supplies, of course.

Probably the most famous cat in advertising is Morris, the finicky feline (actually, a series of look-alike cats), who has pitched 9Lives cat food since 1968. That first Morris was picked out of an Illinois shelter by an advertising executive and turned into an international star. The original

Morris — known to his intimates as Lucky — died in 1975. Actor John Erwin provided the memorable voice for the famous cat — and many other cartoon and live-action characters.

Perhaps not wanting a single cat to increase his feline demands after stardom hit, a competing product went in another direction when choosing cats to pitch products. The catchy "Meow Meow" kitty chorus for Meow Mix is successful because it's hard to get out of your head!

Some of the cats doing incredible things in commercials today aren't real cats at all, but creations of special-effects wizards.

Get the points?

"POINTED CATS"—the Siamese is the best-known example—have solid-color bodies and dark shading on their heads, legs, and tails. Most people know that, but most probably don't know these cats start out white! The body color darkens with age, and most notably the "points" do. Pointed breeds come in a handful of varieties, including:

- Seal: dark brown points on the body ranging from ivory to light brown

- Chocolate: lighter brown points on an ivory body

- Lilac: pinkish gray points on an almost-white body

- Blue: blueish gray points on a lighter gray or ivory body

- Lynx: tabby-marked points of various colors on a lighter body; the body may show faint tabby markings as the cat ages

- Tortie or patched: points of calico on a lighter body

Not all pointed markings are acceptable in the standard for all breeds. For example, Siamese cats can only have points of seal, chocolate, blue, or lilac.

But that was
my favorite sweater!

DOGS WILL CHEW ON almost anything, especially when they're puppies.
Destructive chewing is a common behavior
complaint made by people with dogs, but
there's a destructive chewing problem in some
cats, too.

It's called "wool-sucking" because wool
sweaters, blankets, and more seem to be the most
attractive to cats that have this behavior. (Some
wool-sucking cats prefer plastic materials, such
as those found in a common plastic grocery bag.)
The chewing isn't quite like a dog's total destructive gnaw-it-up: wool-sucking cats typically work
the same spot on a piece of cloth, sucking and

chewing on that one spot and returning to it if distracted.

Some have attributed this behavior to a kitten's being weaned too early, or to the taste of lanolin in wool cloth. In fact, the behavior most likely has a hereditary component, since it's most common in the so-called Oriental breeds such as Siamese or their mixes.

In some cases, more roughage in the diet (such as pureed pumpkin) can reduce a cat's desire to destroy wool clothing and other household items. The best advice, though, is to put away what you don't want the wool-sucker to destroy, and be sure your cat gets enough exercise—the more interactive play the better—to help reduce nervous energy.

Black cats and good luck

IF A BLACK CAT crosses your path, is it bad luck? It depends on where you live. In the United States, it's generally considered to be bad luck. But in England and parts of Continental Europe and Japan, that same black cat crossing in front of you is considered good luck. In England, the bride who sees a black cat when leaving the church will be very lucky in marriage indeed.

Cats, curiosity, and Shakespeare

THE COMMON PHRASE "curiosity killed the cat" has probably been around far longer, but an early version of it is attributed to Shakespeare, who noted that " . . . care [worry] killed a cat" in *Much Ado About Nothing*. Somehow that evolved into "curiosity," although the meaning is largely the same: stick your nose where it doesn't belong, and you can get into trouble.

A more modern usage can be found in the works of both O. Henry and Eugene O'Neill, with the latter credited with the exact phrasing we use today.

Another American playwright, Tennessee Williams, coined one of the most memorable

cat-related adages in the English language, cap-
tured in this exchange between Brick and
Maggie in (of course) *Cat on a Hot Tin Roof*:

Brick: Win what? What is the victory of a cat
on a hot tin roof?

Maggie: Just staying on it, I guess. As long
as she can.

A cat on a hot tin roof is one anxious, un-
happy critter, and the same can be said about
Maggie (the cat) in the play.

The cat from Havana
(not)

UNLIKE THE HAVANESE DOG, which was purportedly the favorite pampered pet of the pre-Castro ruling class, the Havana cat's origins have nothing to do with Cuba.

Instead, the sleek cat with a coat of glossy dark brown was originally called the Havana Brown (and still is in some cat clubs), and the name is said to have been given to it by breed-developers in England and the United States who described the color as that of a good Cuban cigar.

Cats (and other animals) who are uniformly one color are called "self," which basically means "solid." The Russian Blue and black Bombay are other "self-colored" cats.

The feline alphabet

I F YOU LOOK AT your cat's veterinary chart, you'll likely find your pet described either as a DSH or DLH. The letters are veterinary shorthand for "domestic shorthair" or "domestic longhair," respectively. That is, unless your cat is a recognized breed, such as a Persian or Abyssinian, in which case that will be noted instead.

And speaking of terminology, we've always rather liked the British term for a cat of unspecified origins: Moggie. It has a nice, friendly feel to it.

Keeping pace . . . with camels

CATS ARE ONE OF the few animals—camels are another—whose natural gait is the pace. In pacing, the animal's legs on the same side move in unison. Most animals naturally trot, the gait in which legs on the opposite corners—front leg and rear right, front right and rear left—move in unison.

Dogs and horses cover distances at a trot, although—and you're probably ahead of us here—some standardbred racehorses (the kind that pull carts, or sulkies, behind them, no jockeys on top) spend their whole careers pacing. (That's because, although pacing isn't natural and must be taught, it's easier to keep a pacing horse from breaking into a canter or gallop by linking legs on the same side together with leather straps called "hobbles.")

That same pacing gait is what gives the cat that elegant, effortless motion. The fog, as Carl Sandburg wrote, comes in on little cat feet, but when it comes in, it's at a graceful, gliding pace.

Cat shows for the unbreedable

UNLIKE DOG SHOWS, where the animals have to be "intact" to compete, cat shows actively encourage people to get involved with their spayed or neutered pets—even if they're not a recognized breed.

In the breed ranks, altered cats can compete as "premiers." And any well cared-for cat can compete in the "household pet" category, being judged on how overly balanced the animal's appearance is and how well the pet is cared for.

Simple shots?

I N THE 1990S, cat lovers and veterinarians became concerned with "vaccine-related sarcoma"—a type of cancer that seemed to be associated with the preventive-care vaccines given to almost all pet cats. As a result of such incidences, the guidelines for vaccines were overhauled. No longer are "yearly shots" the norm.

Instead, veterinarians now advise clients to tailor a vaccine program to a cat's lifestyle, to split vaccines into separate doses instead of one combination shot, and to give the vaccines at less frequent intervals—as infrequently as every three years.

Since no vaccines are "automatically" given on

an annual basis anymore (except for rabies, which in some locales is required by law every year for the protection of the people, not pets), you'll need to talk to your veterinarian about the right balance between providing your pet with the protection of vaccination without increasing the risk of cancer.

The better to
ear you, my dear

CATS HAVE MORE THAN thirty muscles around each ear to allow them to point the pinna (the visible part of the ear) in the direction of whatever sound they're trying to pick up. The ears can move independently of each other. And, of course, cats have exceptional hearing.

All of this means your cat can hear you just fine — she's just ignoring you.

Calico versus tortoiseshell

ALTHOUGH SOME PEOPLE THINK "calico" and "tortoiseshell" cats are the same thing, in fact they look quite different — although they're genetically similar and almost always female.

Calico cats have black and red/orange patches on a white body. Tortoiseshell cats have no white, and the black and orange are often swirled together.

"Dilute" versions of these cats display the same patterning, except that the red/orange colors are more of a cream, and the black is gray.

As we've mentioned elsewhere in this book, calico and tortoiseshell cats are almost always

female. (In males, the red/orange color is typically displayed only as a tabby.)

The common flea?
It's the cat flea

CATS HAVE CAT FLEAS. So do dogs, usually. In fact, although there are hundreds of species of fleas around the world, it's the cat flea that causes most of the irritation in the United States.

Blaming cats for fleas isn't fair, though. The cat flea got its name because the person who first identified it did so after pulling one off a cat. He could have just as easily pulled one off a dog and given them the blame.

Or maybe, because dogs generally suffer more from fleas than cats do, cats are happy to take credit.

Another annoying parasite, the tick, also isn't

as much of a problem for cats as for dogs, mostly because cats meticulously remove the nasty bloodsuckers while grooming themselves. As if to even things out, though, ear mites seem to really dig cats.

All of these pests are easier and safer to control today than ever before, by the way, so talk to your veterinarian.

Kitty kisses— it's in the eyes

CATS CONSIDER THE straight-on stare of a stranger to be rude at best and threatening at worst. But when it's a person the cat knows, trusts, and likes, direct eye contact can be a kind of nonphysical kitty kiss. See if you can get your cat to try it: look gently into your pet's eyes and slowly blink. Your cat may mimic the behavior, in a kind of "I love you, too" response.

It's a comb,
it's a prey-holder,
it's a bone-cleaner

IF YOU LOOK AT a cat's tongue with a magnifying glass (and good luck trying to do that, by the way!), you'll see it's covered with row after row of barbs. For you scientific types, these little structures that line the surface of a cat's tongue are called *filiform papillae*. They're hooked, and they are directed toward the throat.

These barbs help to hold prey while eating, and they also help a cat keep her fur in perfect (or should we say purrfect?) condition, pulling out dead and dying hairs, along with any debris picked up in the day's travels. Cats can actually feel when a few hairs are out of place, so that tongue is also a convenient, built-in hairbrush.

It's the start of an assembly line for some mighty fine hairballs, as well. Since the hooks direct items down the throat, it's difficult for cats to expel fur objects (or yarn, fishing line, and other things that rightly ought to be expelled) from their mouths. This is one reason cats swallow rather than spit out fur—and then hack it up as hairballs.

Other papillae of the tongue are involved with taste detection. The *filiform papillae* can't taste food, but they do hold food in contact with the tongue long enough to enable the cat to taste it.

Cats can function with no teeth, but they must have at least half their tongue to survive.

Telling temperature by cat

CATS SLEEP IN ONE of two basic positions: upright (think the New York Public Library lions) or on their sides. How curled a cat is when sleeping on her side will depend on how hot or cold the animal is: the more tightly curled a cat is, the colder the air temperature. Curling into a tight ball helps to conserve body heat. When cats stretch out, they expose their bellies, allowing for heat to escape, which helps to cool them.

That said, cats generally like to be warm and will seek out all the warmest places in the home to sleep, as perhaps befitting an animal with roots in the desert.

The tops of televisions (and before that, old cabinet-style radios) have long been popular. More recently, computer monitors are favorites with feline heat-seeking missiles. What's a cat to do now that more and more computer monitors are being replaced with flat-screen displays?

Stretch . . . stretch stretch

WHEN IT COMES TO stretching before any activity, no personal trainer or coach will ever be as committed to the idea as the average cat. When a cat wakes up, she carefully stretches each and every muscle to make sure her strong, supple body is ready for action.

Typically, the stretching routine starts with a good arching of the back and a very, very big yawn. Next is a full-body stretch, right down to the tip of the tail.

We should all be so careful and conscious of

our wonderful bodies as our cats are instinc-tively. We'd be better for it, especially those of us who spend our days working on computers. (Pardon us, we need to stretch now.)

Walking around on needles

YOU DON'T WANT STUDDED snow tires in the middle of the summer, and you only engage four-wheel drive when you need it. Just as snow tires can slow down a car, a cat's claws can slow him down. So the cat retracts them in order to ambulate (a fancy way of saying "walk") without continuously catching his claws. Cat claws come out only when they're needed.

It's a mistake to refer to claws as retractable, by the way. The normal, relaxed position of a cat's claw is retracted, or sheathed. To bring out those daggers, a cat must voluntarily contract muscles and rubber-band-like elastic ligaments underneath her toes. If it was the other way around, the poor cat would have to keep her muscles tensed all day long to keep her claws sheathed.

There is one notable exception in the family of cat: the cheetah. Extended claws help the

cheetah get traction as he sprints after game. The fastest land animal, the cheetah's top speed of more than seventy miles per hour can only be maintained for two hundred to three hundred yards before the cat must chill. With luck, he has already caught his dinner.

Pounce percentages

A CAT HAS A POUNCING average that a Major League baseball player would envy. About one pounce in three ends up with dinner—that's batting .333! How do cats learn to hunt? All that crazy kitten play, pouncing on bugs and chasing dust bunnies, is practice for grown-up hunting.

Mom helps, too. Cats have a genetic predisposition to kill things (after all, cats *are* carnivores), but they also learn from watching Mom, who teaches them how to whip up a dish of Mice-a-Roni from something the cats dragged in.

Cats and dogs together — a world gone mad!

WHILE THE IDEA OF dogs and cats at war with each other is a comedic staple, 47 percent of people who share their homes with a cat also have a dog. These pets get along to varying degrees, from out-and-out loathing to familial affection. If properly (as in slowly, at the animals' own speed) introduced, dogs and cats usually at least tolerate each other well.

More households have dogs, by the way, but there are more pet cats in the United States. How is that possible? More dogs are "only children," while the average number of cats kept in the average household has increased to nearly 2.5. That figure more reflects the ease of caring for a cat—or the perception of easy care—than the interest cats have in sharing space.

Unless raised together as kittens, many cats would prefer to remain the only cat in a given home. That's quite different from dogs, who as pack animals generally enjoy the company of their own kind.

A new way to deal with an old problem

EVERY COMMUNITY HAS what are called feral cats—abandoned pets and their offspring. Although many people figure cats can take care of themselves and dump their pets when they no longer want them, the fact is that the lives of feral cats are full of danger and fear—and often those nine lives tick off faster than the sweeping hand of a stopwatch.

There have always been kindhearted people who feed homeless cats, even if it's just sharing a tuna sandwich from a park bench. There have also always been people who find colonies of feral cats to be annoying: the cats make noise, spray urine, and multiply like . . . well . . . cats.

There was a time when municipalities handled feral cat colonies by putting out poison or trapping all the cats and dropping them off at the

local shelter—whether they were adoptable or not. More recently, though, the trend has been toward a more humane way to handle feral cats called TNR, which stands for "trap, neuter, and return."

TNR advocates argue that just feeding feral cats makes the problem worse, but that trapping and killing the cats doesn't solve the problem in the long run.

Instead, they trap the cats, place the ones they can in caring homes, and return the rest after they've been neutered and immunized. These colonies can then be fed and cared for in a hands-off but humane way, and their numbers dwindle naturally because the reproductive taps have been turned off for good.

Trap, neuter, and return programs for feral cats seem counterintuitive to many people. If you don't want cats around, wouldn't it make sense just to remove them permanently? As it turns out . . . no.

When you remove cats, other animals take their place. That's because the food source that attracted the cats will still be there, which means more cats (or rats or coyotes or raccoons) will eventually show up. Meanwhile, studies have shown that trapping feral cats, finding homes for the ones you can, and neutering the rest before returning them to their colonies really does reduce their numbers.

Neutering reduces the fighting, yowling, and spraying behaviors, many of which are associated with fighting over mates. The neutered cats defend their territory, too, and prevent other animals from moving in—including unneutered cats. Think of them as flashing furry gang colors, ready to make war but unable to make love. (The colony caretakers are quick to remove and find homes for any abandoned pets who turn up, as well as any kittens.)

While such programs aren't perfect—and aren't considered appropriate for locations where the protection of small prey species is necessary—they have been shown to be both more humane and more effective than past efforts to simply exterminate feral cats.

Up, up, and rarely away: how cats get stuck in trees

CAT CLAWS ARE DESIGNED to move a cat forward, anchoring her as she propels herself. If that forward direction is up a tree, it's difficult to head back down. Instead, the gracefully powerful movement of a cat heading up a tree is counterbalanced by the crashing and (if she's lucky) controlled free fall she'll use to get down.

Most cats do find their way back down, of course, which is a good thing these days. With municipal budgets being what they are, few fire departments are allowed to respond to "cat stuck in tree" calls anymore.

We don't recommend that you get out that tall

ladder, either. You have a better chance of getting seriously hurt while reaching for a scared cat—and scared cats aren't safe to handle, even if they're yours—than your cat does of getting injured when she decides it's time to head down for dinner. You may be able to whet her appetite by opening a can of tuna, salmon, or mackerel, and letting the wonderful fishy smell drift upward.

Let me lick you

CATS LICK THEMSELVES CLEAN right after dinner because instinct has taught them the sooner they remove food odors, the less likely that predators will get a whiff of McCat. Your cat will often lick you after you get out of the shower for a variation of the same reason — you don't smell right, and your cat is trying to fix that.

A cat is a cat is a cat, for all that

WHEN YOU THINK ABOUT all the variation we've bred into dogs—they're all the same species still, from Mastiff to Maltese—isn't it a tad odd that we haven't fussed with the basic size and shape of a cat very much?

Among cat breeds, the size variation ranges from five to around twenty pounds. (In dogs, it ranges from less than five to more than two hundred pounds.) From the smallest cat to the biggest, some cats are bulkier than others, but they're still basically shaped like cats. (In dogs, consider the difference between the greyhound and the dachshund, or the whippet and the English bulldog. Heck, even collies come in two varieties: long-haired "Lassie types" and short-haired "smooth types.")

About the only real variation in body shape are the higher rumps of tailless breeds like the Manx and Japanese Bobtail. Unless, that is, you count the controversial Munchkin, a cat with a genetic mutation that gives the animal short legs like a Basset Hound—but gives many cat lovers fits to think about.

Thanks, but I don't want your mouse

LOVERS BRING CHOCOLATES; cats bring mice. We all have our own way of saying, "I love you." And consider this: cats don't bring you *any old* dead mice. No! These are mice they have hunted and killed themselves.

There's something about the thrill of the hunt that stirs even the best-fed cat to stalk, chase, and pounce. But only love will inspire her to share.

If you're not understanding enough to realize that the occasional headless mouse in bed is a gift of true respect and admiration—not to mention a tasty treat your cat wants you to eat!—well, we're not sure you're truly cat-lover material.

Dead critters are bad enough, of course, but what about those cats who bring in the mortally wounded? Then you have a cat who really, *really* loves you. Not only is she making sure you don't starve, but she's trying her best to make sure you understand how to feed yourself—and are entertained as well. It's your turn to play with the prey. Don't you just love a cat who shares her toys?

Now, before you get rid of that mouse or finch, put on some gloves. You never know what vile disease that critter may be harboring.

Kitties on the go?

CATS GENERALLY DON'T LIKE riding in cars, although those who've been acclimated to travel from kittenhood can learn to tolerate it well enough.

The reason most cats would rather stay home? Actually, there are a couple reasons. First, cats thrive on routine and the familiar smells of their own territory. Being put into a car is a definite break in routine and, sure as all get-out, it's not familiar territory from the minute you leave home.

Then, consider that most times when cats go

anywhere, the destination isn't one they'd choose—the veterinary hospital.

Add it all up and you can imagine why some cats go into hiding when they see the carrier come out.

A change of names

WHILE A MALE CAT—especially an unneutered one—is today called a "tom," that wasn't always the case. Up until the late 1700s, male cats were known as "rams" (like sheep) or "boars" (like pigs). A book about cats with a character named Tom became popular in the latter part of the century; after that, male cats started being called tomcats.

Everyone loves a kitten, but nobody wants a cat

I N SHELTERS ACROSS the country, adult cats find it very difficult to find new homes. That's because they're competing with one of nature's most adorable creatures—kittens!

And that's sad, because many of these adult cats would make absolutely wonderful pets if someone—anyone—would just give them a chance. They've mellowed beyond the crazy kitten stage, they're more able to spend time alone while you're at work, and yet they're happy to be your loving companion.

Adult cats at the height of kitten season—late summer and early fall—have little to no chance of competing with the flood of fluffy babies.

Even all the kittens won't find homes. (We can't think of a better argument for spay-neuter!)

In the winter, when kittens are few and far between, adult cats fare a little better on the adoption front.

What does that mean to you? If you're looking for a pet, consider a healthy, well-mannered adult cat. And if you're thinking of giving up your cat, please work on resolving the problems instead, because there's unlikely to be a home for the pet you're dumping.

Kitties get wheezy, too

STRANGE AS IT MAY seem, cats get asthma, too.

The signs of asthma in cats are very similar to those seen in humans—difficulty breathing, first and foremost. Cats with asthma also "wheeze" and may exhibit a cough that sometimes sounds like gagging. If he's having trouble breathing, a cat sits with his neck extended, and inhales and exhales rapidly with his mouth open. Sometimes people hear a coughing cat and think "hairball" when they really should think "asthma."

Or rather, they should think "veterinarian," because there are more reasons than asthma why a cat would have problems breathing, and a veterinarian's help is needed to get a good diagnosis. Once you know your cat's an asthmatic, your veterinarian will help you keep your pet breathing freely—and no, it won't require your cat to carry around an inhaler like the wheezing kid you knew—or were—in grade school.

Another common human illness that seems to be on the rise in cats is diabetes. Perhaps not surprisingly, it's linked to an increase in the rates of obesity in both humans and cats.

The extrasensory cat

TWO PHENOMENA THAT HAVE been well-documented over the years suggest that cats have a few more things going for them than we mere humans can understand.

One of these is the ability to "predict" seismic events, such as earthquakes. Cats (and other animals) appear to be sensitive to signs of increasing tension below the ground, a theory promoted by those who claim that before an earthquake, the number of lost cats and dogs increases—presumably because the animals are attempting to escape from any danger.

Another interesting skill is the cat's ability to

return to what he recognizes as "home" from hundreds of miles away—after his family moves, for example. Although some of these cases are surely mistaken identity on the part of the people and cats involved, others are well-documented, and experiments have shown that cats have a particular sensitivity to the earth's magnetic field and so are masters of direction—no road maps needed.

The nose knows

HUMANS HAVE FINGERPRINTS; cats have noses. The pattern of skin on a cat's nose is unique. No cat will have a pattern that exactly matches the nose of another.

He really was the cat's pajamas

THE TERM "CAT'S PAJAMAS" comes from an English tailor of the late 1700s and early 1800s who made the finest silk pajamas for royalty and other rich patrons. His name was E. B. Katz.

The End

About the Authors

Dr. Marty Becker

As a veterinarian, media personality, author, and educator, Dr. Marty Becker has become known as the "best-loved family doctor for pets."

Marty is the popular veterinary contributor to ABC-TV's *Good Morning, America* and the host of *The Pet Doctor* on PBS. He is also the coauthor (with Gina Spadafori) of the "Pet Connection," a popular feature syndicated to newspapers and websites internationally through Universal Press Syndicate. He has appeared on Animal Planet and is a frequent guest on national network and cable television, as well as radio shows. He has

been interviewed for countless magazine and
newspaper articles.

Marty is an adjunct professor at his alma
mater, Washington State University College of
Veterinary Medicine, and at the Colorado State
University College of Veterinary Medicine. He
has lectured at every veterinary school in the
United States and been named Companion
Animal Veterinarian of the Year by the Delta
Society and the American Veterinary Medical
Association.

Marty is coauthor of the fastest-selling pet
book in history, *Chicken Soup for the Pet Lover's Soul,*
and is either sole author or coauthor of other top-
selling books, including other animal books in
the *Chicken Soup* line, *The Healing Power of Pets:
Harnessing the Amazing Ability of Pets to Make and
Keep People Happy and Healthy,* and *Fitness
Unleashed! A Dog and Owner's Guide to Losing Weight*

and Gaining Health Together! With Gina Spadafori, he has authored *Why Do Dogs Drink Out of the Toilet? 101 of the Most Perplexing Questions Answered About Canine Conundrums, Medical Mysteries and Befuddling Behaviors* (a *New York Times* bestseller) and *Do Cats Always Land on Their Feet? 101 of the Most Perplexing Questions Answered About Feline Unfathomables, Medical Mysteries, and Befuddling Behaviors.* The pair collaborated with Teresa Becker and Audrey Pavia on *Why Do Horses Sleep Standing Up? 101 of the Most Perplexing Questions Answered About Equine Enigmas, Medical Mysteries, and Befuddling Behaviors.*

Marty devotes his life to his family, which includes his beloved wife, Teresa, daughter, Mikkel, and son, Lex, along with all the furry family members on the Beckers' Almost Heaven Ranch in northern Idaho.

Gina Spadafori

Gina Spadafori has been blessed with the opportunity to combine two of her dearest loves—animals and words—into a career writing about animals. Since 1984, she has written an award-winning weekly column on pets and their care.

Gina has served on the boards of directors of both the Cat Writers Association (CWA) and the Dog Writers Association of America (DWAA). She has won the DWAA's Maxwell Medallion for the best newspaper column, and her column has also been honored with a certificate of excellence by the CWA. The first edition of her top-selling book, *Dogs for Dummies,* was given the President's Award for the best writing on dogs and the Maxwell Medallion for the best general reference work, both by the DWAA.

In addition to *Dogs for Dummies* and the books

written with Dr. Becker, Gina has coauthored other award-winning books. Along with Dr. Paul D. Pion, a top veterinary cardiologist, she was given the CWA's awards for the best work on feline nutrition, best work on feline behavior, and best work on responsible cat care for the top-selling *Cats for Dummies*. The book was named one of the hundred best feline moments in the twentieth century by *Cat Fancy* magazine. With avian specialist Dr. Brian L. Speer, Gina wrote *Birds for Dummies*, one of the best-selling books on pet birds ever written.

Gina has also headed one of the first and largest online pet-care sites, the Pet Care Forum, America Online's founding source of pet-care information.

Gina lives in northern California in a decidedly multispecies home.

Index

acting roles, 116, 136
ailurophobia (*see* cat phobia)
All-American Maine Coon, 67–68
American Association of Feline Practitioners (AAFP), 124
asthma, 190–191

Bialik, Carl, 106
Black Bombay, 146
black cats, 142
blood transfusions, 34–36
bones, 50–51
Braun, Lilian Jackson, 121
Breakfast at Tiffany's, 116
breeding, 98–100, 181–182

calico, 19, 52, 154
Cat Behavior, 135
Cat on a Hot Tin Roof, 144
cat phobias, 109
cat worship, 39–40
catnip, 12, 29–31
Catworld: A Feline Encyclopedia, 7
chattering, 46
cheetah, 79, 167–168
Churchill, Winston, 120
claws, 166–168
climbing, 45, 177–178
Colby Nolan, 32–33
Collector's Hold Museum Putty, 38
Cornish Rex, 57, 94

Devon Rex, 57
diabetes, 191
dietary habits, 9, 83–84, 96, 102
dogs, living with, 170
domestication, 157 42–43

ear mites,

eating grass, 11
Egypt, 39, 42, 133
Erwin, John, 137
eye color, 74–75
eye contact, 158

feline lower urinary tract disease (FLUTD), 14–15
feral cats, 173–176
fighting behavior, 101
fleas, 155
Freya, 40

Giannelli, David, 118
ginger toms, 20, 53
grooming, 61–62, 114–115

hair, 94
hairballs, 48–49, 160
Havana Brown, 146
Hayes, Rutherford B., 131
heads, shape, 24
hearing, 69–70, 71, 153
heart rate, 3–4
hiding behavior, 28
Himmy, 81
Homeward Bound, 117
hunting, 104, 169, 183–184

introduction to United States, 26

Japanese Bobtail, 50, 57, 182
jumping, 80

Katz, E. B., 195
Klinefelter syndrome, 53
kneading behavior, 85

Lady and the Tramp, 132

licking, 22, 180
lions, 88
litter box problems, 14
litter, largest, 86
mackerel tabby, 20
Maine Coon Cat, 24, 56, 66–68
Manx, 50, 182
Meet the Parents, 117
Morris the Cat, 136–137
Morris, Desmond, 7
Much Ado About Nothing, 143
mummified, 39
Munchkin, 182
naming, 121

Near Eastern wildcat, 43
neutering, 22, 73, 175, 187, 189
nose skin pattern, 194
Norwegian Forest Cats, 56

O. Henry, 143
O'Neill, Eugene, 143
Orangey, 116

parenting, 128–130
Patsy Awards, 116
Pepper, 116
Persians, 24, 94, 127
personality types, 127
points, 138–139
purring, 6–8

QuakeHold! 38

Ragdolls, 56
religious depictions, 126
respiration rate, 4
rubbing, 21
Russian Blue, 146

Sassy, 117
Shakespeare, William, 143
shows, 150

Siam (*also* Thailand), 39
Siamese, 24, 127, 131–132, 138
Siberians, 56
Singapura, 56
sleep, 1, 92–93, 162–163
speed, 78–79
spaying, 106–108, 135, 150, 189
Sphynx, 111–112
spraying, 22, 72–73
stretching, 164–165

tabby, 18–19, 53–54, 63–64
Tabor, Roger, 135
tapetum lucidum, 58–59
taste, 9–10
taurine, 96
temperature, 4
territorial behavior, 134–135
ticks, 156–157
tiger, 8, 18, 61, 63
toes, 44–45
tomcats, 73, 89, 187
tongue, 159–160
tortoiseshells, 19, 52, 154
Towser, 104
traveling, 185–186
trichobezoar (*see* hairballs)
Trinity Southern University, 32
Turkish Vans, 56

vaccination, 151–152
valerian, 12, 30–31
veterinarian specialty, 123–124
vision, 58–60

weight, 56, 81
whiskers, 90–91
white cats, 71, 75
Williams, Tennessee, 143
wool sucking, 140–141

zoomies, 16

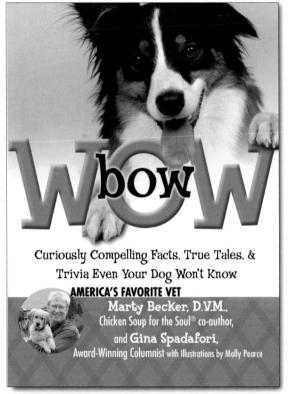